RICHARD A. VAUGHAN

THE
100 TON
CHALLENGE

LESSONS LEARNED FROM LIFTING 13 ELEPHANTS AND A BOEING 737 WITH YOUR MIND, BODY AND HEART

PREFACE

Special thanks to my lovely wife Catherine, who is a very loving person with a great heart; and, of course, my training partners, son Matthew, son-in-law Colin, and dear friend Dana Cooper, a guy who has helped me both physically (especially on the road bike) and spiritually throughout the years and who continues to be an inspiration.

Thanks also to my extended family – former wife Margie, daughter Kelsey (my special K) and my son Matthew, along with my brother Bill and sister Mary – for putting up with me over many years of my unique adventures.

Lifelong injuries and challenges that life gave me to appreciate what I do have and to remind me to always improvise, adapt and overcome:

- Four broken fingers, two on each hand
- Broken left ankle that resulted in a plate and three screws to keep it together
- Fractures in both ankles, torn ligaments, calcium deposits, and bone spurs
- Broken nose
- Fractured jaw
- Fracture boned in left wrist, twice in same bone
- Torn meniscus, left knee
- Torn rotator cuff, right shoulder
- Fractured collarbone
- Five cracked ribs
- Herniated disk in lower back, then fractured disk in L4/5 area, missing part of disk from surgery
- Plastic surgery and a total 800 stitches in my facial area along with replacement of my front tooth
- Neuropathy in both feet

Table of Contents

Introduction 1

Chapter 1 5
The Why: Inspiration and Purpose

Chapter 2 17
Scarred for Life and Challenges Along the Way:
Try Using the Kintsugi Philosophy

Chapter 3 27
The Strategy: How to Attack a Seemingly Impossible Feat
with Training and Preparation

Chapter 4 39
Don't Ever Give Up...Simply Reset!

Chapter 5 51
The Results and What's Next

Appendix 69
The Magic Formula for Lifting Those 13 Elephants
or a Boeing 737 Airliner

INTRODUCTION

THE 100-TON CHALLENGE:

Life provides countless challenges and obstacles as we journey through our personal and professional lives. These hurdles may be physical, mental, emotional, or spiritual and can occur at any age. To cope, we may need to call upon a variety of resources and remedies. My own journey has often been interrupted by significant traumatic physical challenges, along with experiences that provided the kind of life lessons that scarred me, but in a beneficial way.

Sometimes I can be hardheaded, so it has taken some significant impacts for me to wake-up when I needed to alter my course. Yet, no matter how painful, the results of these blows have always been combined with honest reflections that provided true-life educational moments along the way. The 100-Ton Challenge had that effect on me. This event involved lifting 200,000 pounds in 24 hours which is the approximate weight of 13 elephants or a Boeing 737 airliner! It was a dynamic metaphor for doing something perceived as impossible but with the proper mindset, training, strategy, discipline, and a strong will to achieve could have amazing results...and I was especially interested to see what a 66-year-old body could achieve!

The added ingredients of this event's appeal were motivation, inspiration and a heartfelt desire to pay it forward. When I started the challenge, I was semi-retired and, truthfully, retirement was wearing on me. I had lost some spark in my life, boredom had set in, and I needed new challenges. Aging is not for the weak, so I thought about what I could do to regain the eye of the tiger and focus on new goals. Experimenting is a good way to discover new talents. So, I learned to test my creativity and took up crafting mosaic-tile projects with various desert and landscaping scenes, thanks to my mentors Roni Thomas and Buck Marsala who are true artists and helped me discover a new artistic skill set.

Working out at the gym and maintaining a level of fitness had always been part of my life, and I gravitated toward that interest when I truly had more time to dedicate toward various hobbies. The physical demands of the 100-Ton Challenge had piqued my interest, and I had discovered the Gary Sinise Foundation, an amazing nonprofit that builds homes for severely disabled veterans, among other programs to honor our veterans. Plus, I had started thinking about how cool it would be to somehow honor my dad, who was a highly decorated veteran.

Taking on a physical challenge and leveraging it to raise money to help others was really appealing and created a new mission for me. Although I had never written a book, I took on writing as another adventure. I thought I could weave in my personal challenges, the legendary and inspirational stories about my dad's military service and draw some analogies from those experiences to possibly inspire other people to go beyond their comfort zones and achieve some level of success in their own lives.

I share these stories, challenges, and inspirations to hopefully provide a road map to anyone interested in achieving something perceived as overwhelmingly unlikely, improbable, or even impossible. I say, dare to prove them wrong!

CHAPTER 1

The Why: Inspiration & Purpose

I had read an article in The Wall Street Journal about a San Antonio Military Base where retired and active-duty veterans work out and once a year host a challenge event where they attempt to lift 100 tons (200,000 pounds) in one day. Wow…I wondered how that was possible. These veterans were lifting the equivalent of 13 elephants or a 737 Boeing Airliner!

INSPIRATION:

Creating a purpose, or having a goal, helps motivation.

I decided to go for the 100-Ton Challenge. What inspiration did I use to tackle this seemingly impossible feat? Could I use it to benefit others? Let's start with my inspiration and later explore how I could use this action to benefit others.

My dad was my hero. When I was a kid and a teenager, he went to all my baseball games and wrestling matches. He made sure that I toed the line and gave me a little tough love when needed. He provided an example of why character and integrity are important, ensuring that my siblings and I were respectful to our mother and other people along the way. He taught us the value of being independent and allowed us to make our own decisions while being accountable for the consequences.

The path was not always smooth. I distinctly remember my older brother seemed to get into a lot of trouble and hung out with some unsavory characters. We grew up in the Midwest, outside of Youngstown, Ohio, a steel town made up of primarily middle-class Americans, blue collar neighborhoods but there were some tough aspects as well. One day etched in my mind made it clear to my twin brother Bill and me that dad was not someone to be messed with.

We were playing in the house and heard noises outside. We peeked out our front window to see my older brother scrambling from his car as four tough-looking gang-member types pulled up our driveway, jumped out of their car, and approached the house. My older brother screamed for dad while trying to explain that these guys with knives were threatening him. Dad told him to wait in the house and grabbed his favorite hickory axe-handle before stepping onto the front porch to confront these scary-looking dudes. Our eyes were as big as saucers as my twin and I looked at each other and wondered what was going to happen now!

Four against one were not good odds but dad seemed perfectly calm with no sign of fear. We lived in a close-knit neighborhood where hard-working blue-collar types lived and raised their families. One of our neighbors, a contractor and cement mason, must have been watching the scene at our house because he suddenly stormed out of his front door with a sledgehammer in hand and ran across the street to see how he could help.

We never found out exactly what was said, but those hoodlums left in a hurry. They must have realized it probably was unwise to tangle with these tough old veterans who had seen major combat in WWII and were not going to be intimidated, that it was best for their own health to back off. Wow...it was like a scene from the movies.

Afterward, my older brother was restricted to the house for two weeks and got a couple whacks across his backside. And we all began to understand that there might be more to dad's history. We had no idea until many years later when we learned about his incredible WWII record and experiences.

Dad's story came to light in 2009 when I was asked to attend a ceremony to induct him into the Ohio Military Hall of Fame. He was to be recognized as one of the most highly decorated veterans in the history of the state of Ohio. The ultimate tribute happened many years later on August 29, 2022, when the Ohio State Congress and Assembly passed a bill that dedicated a bridge (right outside our hometown, Austintown, Ohio, over Route 46) to be named in honor of dad for his outstanding WWII record and service to our country.

As stated in the ceremony to honor my dad:

> "William Vaughan was born on August 14th, 1920. He graduated from Austintown Fitch in 1938. He enlisted in the Army Air Force on 13 November 1941 three weeks before Pearl Harbor. He attained the Rank of T/Sgt. and then 2nd Lieutenant. He was a radio operator and gunner on the B-17 E model and served two tours in the Pacific for a total of 24 months. He flew 73 combat missions and 594 combat hours with the 5th Air Force and the 19th and then the 43rd bomb group based in Australia. He was shot down and wounded on a bombing run over Rabaul when they engaged 10 Japanese Zero's and landed 300 yards offshore with three other crewmen and were found by friendly natives and worked their way through enemy lines to an Aussie camp and then rejoined his outfit. He also was part of an advanced landing party of a couple of B-17's and some Australian troops to get an old landing strip ready at Milne Bay when 700 to 1,000 Japanese who landed a
>
> few miles away attacked the party. They knew they were coming and removed their 50-caliber guns from the airplanes and opened up when they were 150 yards away. The battle lasted for 8 hours and both sides began to run out of ammunition and the

Japanese charged. Vaughan took out two with the last two rounds of his 45 then he eliminated two with his jungle knife. Estimated a total of 10-12 kills. He received a bayonet slash on his neck. They also left formation on a bombing run over Wewak to take out lots of search lights saving their planes from anti-aircraft fire.

Vaughan was part of the most decorated flight crew in Air Force history or any branch of service to this day and there is a display in the Museum of the Air Force at Wright Patterson Air Force Base in Dayton, Ohio. They were on a mapping mission over the Solomon Islands to film the coral reefs for an invasion when 15 Japanese Zero's attacked, and they couldn't turn because the camera was running and fought them off until they finished. It was an all-volunteer crew and was called a suicide mission. The B-17E 41-2666 was named old 666 then renamed Lucy and received 187 7.7-millimeter holes and 5 20-millimeter cannon holes. The crew received 2 Medals of Honor and 7 Distinguished Service Crosses and 4 Purple hearts. Vaughan was hit in the neck with a bullet fragment. The pilot became the most decorated pilot in Air Force history. These are just a few of the highlights of his service to this country. He is one of the most decorated Veterans in Mahoning County and is in the Ohio Military Hall of Fame for Valor. He became a 2nd Lieutenant when he came back after 24 months in the Pacific to attend flight school to become a Bombardier."

William Vaughan's Military Awards
- Distinguished Service Cross
- Silver Star
- Distinguished Flying Cross
- Purple Hearts (3), flack fragment, bayonet wound, bullet fragment, all in the neck
- Air Medals (14)
- Two Presidential Unit Citations: Java, Singapore, and Rabaul
- Southwest Pacific Campaign Ribbon with five campaign stars. Coral Sea, Papuan, Milne Bay, Midway, and Burma
- American Defense Ribbon
- Good Conduct Ribbon
- Philippine Campaign Ribbon
- 73 combat missions in a B-17 with a total of 594 combat hours
- Radio operator and top gunner credited with nine planes shot down and four probables
- In 1944 he became a 2nd Lieutenant and got his pilot wings as a Bombardier

There is a book called "The Lucky 666, The Impossible Mission," by Bob Drury and Tom Clavin, about the most decorated mission in the history of the U.S. Air Force. My dad happened to be part of that crew. This too served as my motivation and inspiration to tackle something perceived as impossible…lifting 100 tons (200,000 pounds) in 24 hours. But let's be real…I was not being shot at and flying above enemy territory while navigating over 1,200 miles of shark-infested South Pacific waters. :)

The highest U.S. military award and honor received is the Medal of Honor designation. The captain of the crew of my dad's B-17, Jay Zeamer, was a recipient of that medal. When dad passed away in 1999, my stepmother Vi received this letter in the mail from Captain Zeamer:

"Dear Vi,

It was a total shock when I learned of Willy's (that's the name he gave to dad) passing.

I owe my life and the lives of our entire crew to Willy. I never forgot how he came forward with his shirt covered with blood and saw that we had no navigation, and all the navigation instruments were shot out of the panel and were hanging down on their wires and that all we had left was a magnetic compass. And he went back to his station and set up an old liaison radio, which he liked to play with because all his regular radios were shot out. Then, by Morse code, he contacted the radio station at Dobodura and had them take a radio bearing on us. And he came back up to the cockpit and handed me a small piece of paper that said simply "247-degree M." This enabled me, after a couple of hours, to get in sight of the runway at Dobodura just before I went blind and passed out from loss of blood.

- Barbara and I both join you with our deepest sympathy and our prayers.

Fondly, Jay

A son can have no greater inspiration.

Another powerful inspiration to achieve something that seemed impossible came from my great-grandfather, Thomas Vaughan. While growing up I thought my great-grandfather was my grandfather, but I later in life learned that my dad's real father had abandoned him, and my great-grandfather had raised my dad.

Thomas Vaughan was a Welsh citizen who had worked in the coal mines in southern Wales. He later immigrated to the U.S. and worked on the railroads in the Midwest. He was one tough hombre! I remember he always liked to kick a football around with us, although I never thought much of it until I learned he was an accomplished rugby player back in Wales, where he lived in a small town called Blaina. In fact, I inherited his Championship Caps, which was a tradition in rugby back in 1897-98 and 1901-02.

Why was I inspired to try something as crazy as lifting 200,000 pounds in 24 hours? I distinctly remembered a day in my youth when this old man, my great-grandfather (who was 80 years old at the time), came over to our house to help my dad move 10 tons of slag (large, one-inch-thick rock) to lay a foundation for a new concrete porch in our backyard. The only problem was my dad had become rather ill and was bedridden for a few days. So, this 80-year-old man wheelbarrowed 10 tons of rock, by himself, around to the back yard. He was tireless and methodical in his approach, and with dogged perseverance finished the project, and drove off at the end of the day in his 1948 Hudson. That was quite inspiring and a vivid illustration of how one person can achieve amazing things at any age!

Which reminds me of a funny anecdote: My son Matthew always remembered that story about his Great-Great Grandfather. So when he was about 26 years old, he heard I had ordered 10 tons of decorative rock delivered to our house to be spread over our front and side yards. I had planned to spread the rock that weekend when I got home from a business trip. Upon my return, I discovered that my son had secretly come over the house and spent the whole day spreading the rock by himself, matching my great-grandfather's feat, only 50 years later!

PURPOSE:

I dedicated the first 100-Ton Challenge to my dad and honored him by raising monies for veterans through the Gary Sinise Foundation. This organization helps build homes for returning disabled veterans and honors those men and women who served. Gary Sinise (award-winning American actor who played Lt. Dan in the movie *Forest Gump* and starred on the TV show CSI: NY) outlined the purpose of his foundation like this:

> "We serve our nation by honoring our defenders, veterans, first responders, their families, and those in need. We do this by creating and supporting unique programs designed to entertain, educate, inspire, strengthen, and build communities. Freedom and security are precious gifts that we, as Americans, should never take for granted. We must do all we can to extend our hand in times of need to those who

willingly sacrificed each day to provide that freedom and security. While we can never do enough to show gratitude to our nation's defenders, we can always do a little more."

Today, we glorify athletes and celebrities because of their athletic achievements or stardom status. But I revere the men and women who willingly sacrificed their lives for a greater cause…to protect our freedoms, our security, and our democracy. This was my inspiration and focus for achieving the 100-Ton Challenge on my dad's birthday, August 14, and my birthday, August 15, as a small way to give back.

Everyone needs support and extra motivation to tackle a deed of this magnitude. So, I asked my son Matthew and good friend Dana Cooper along with my son-in-law Colin Buchanan to join me on this quest, which meant they also would have to lift 100 tons (200,000 pounds) each! We would be the two old guys with the two young bucks. :)

I organized a second 100-Ton Challenge and dedicated it to laid-off hospitality and tourism workers in Tucson. This project was also very dear to my heart. My career in the hotel and destination marketing arena spanned 40 years. I had a deep appreciation for the hard work all frontline hospitality employees provide to ensure satisfied customers and contribute to a robust $2.5 billion economy in Tucson. The local hospitality industry was devastated by COVID-19, and we saw millions of people nationally lose their jobs or be laid off due to the economic downturn caused by the pandemic.

My heart sank deeper thinking of all those tourism-based careers being eliminated and the hardships endured by those individuals and families impacted by this destructive disease. It especially hit home during the holidays, so I thought we could do something to ease the pain and provide a little cash to those in need over the Christmas holidays coming up.

As you can see, my inspiration and purpose were powerful. We all face many obstacles throughout our lives that can seem overwhelming. It behooves us to think differently as we deal with these challenges. Anger can be a motivating force as we dwell on the hand being dealt to us, but my advice is to rechannel negative feelings and, instead, be reinvigorated by motivation and inspiration. My personal motivations were right in front of me, so probably easier for me to fixate on. But there were other times in my life – such as when I was faced with overwhelming physical and health challenges – that anger and raw emotions surfaced. I found out quickly that I needed to reframe those thoughts to a more positive mindset if I was to survive.

CHAPTER 2

Scarred for Life and Challenges Along the Way... Try Using the Kintsugi Philosophy

Candice Kumai wrote the beautiful and thoughtful book, "Kintsugi Wellness...The Japanese Art of Nourishing Mind, Body and Spirit." In this book, she explains:

> "The Japanese art form kintsugi is the art of repairing broken vessels by sealing the cracks with lacquer and carefully dusted gold, silver, or platinum.

The Japanese believe the golden cracks make the pieces even more precious and valuable. Kintsugi teaches you that your broken pieces make you stronger and better than ever. When you think you are broken, you can pick up the pieces, put them back together, and learn to embrace the cracks. Kintsugi teaches us that we are more beautiful for our flaws, our battle scars, our lessons learned. I learned that many of us feel broken or damaged or simply not good enough. Too much of the time we are so busy being hard on ourselves that it is easy to lose sight of the fact that we are also deserving of the self-care it takes to maintain our health and happiness."

Spring 1996 was going to be my kintsugi milestone and time to overcome some overwhelming odds in my life. I was trying to park my car after dropping off my kids and wife at the entrance to the Birmingham, Alabama airport before we left for a cruise with the grandparents and extended family members. This was to be the start of a different adventure in my life. My son wanted to go with me to park the car, but I asked him to stay with his mother and help with the luggage. Ultimately, that one decision served to save the life of my son that day.

It was a beautiful, sunny morning as I pulled away from the departing area and went to find a long-term parking facility. I had to recircle the airport to get back to the road that would take me there. As I was making a left turn to get back on the correct road, I quickly realized I had not looked long enough to my right to avoid being hit by an oncoming truck traveling at about 50 miles per hour and then…BOOM!

The weird part is before the impact I was aware that something was very wrong, a sixth sense type of thing. I knew I was about to be blindsided by something large, and my wife was going to be a little upset that we may be late for our flight to Florida that would take us on a family cruise. After the crash, it was eerily quiet and seemed like everything was happening in slow motion. I felt nothing and suddenly realized I was trying to crawl out of my Volvo station wagon, which had been hurled 25 yards down a median to the right side of the road. My body was lying in a field, and I was not sure how I got there.

I recognized sirens in the background and became disoriented. Then I felt a sheet being pulled over me. I still felt no pain but, out of the corner of my eye, I saw massive amounts of blood around the scene. I began to hear muffled voices saying something like "no one could have survived that crash" and I was aware of commotion and people scrambling around me. Finally, I realized I was being put on a gurney to be lifted up into an ambulance. Once I was in the ambulance, I heard the ER guys saying I was going into shock and my body temperature was dropping rapidly.

This was serious but I felt surprisingly calm. Of course, I soon began to understand the severity of the situation. It was kind of crazy, but my thoughts drifted to a book I had recently read on the life of Chuck Norris, the actor and martial arts/karate champion. I had practiced a variety of martial art forms myself over the years, and the book described an incident I could relate to at that moment. Norris had become gravely ill, and his body was breaking down, his temperature plummeting, and he was going into shock. Yet he somehow focused on willing his body to raise its temperature and warm itself. I am not sure how scientific this was, but I thought…what the hell, I have to do something…even though it seemed preposterous or impossible given the condition I was in.

Suddenly, I heard the ER personnel say that I was stabilizing, and they needed to get me into the trauma unit STAT/ASAP. The trauma unit and personnel at the Brookwood hospital in Birmingham, Alabama were excellent and very responsive to my critical injuries. I was able to hear some conversations and actually tilted my head to see one of the nurses look away in horror after seeing the damage done to my face once the sheet was lifted off my head. This quickly crystallized for me the fact that I had been thrown through the windshield and rattled back inside the car; thus, the damage done by the force and the shattered glass was severe.

Fortunately for me, there just happened to be one of the best plastic surgeons on call that day, and he got to me quickly. He spoke with me in a supportive and calm manner, but was honest and said, "This is going to be tough because in order to perform the plastic surgery needed on my face correctly, you will have to stay awake for the duration of the process." Seven hours and 680 stitches later, I was out of surgery. I was just glad the surgeon was an avid golfer because he talked to me about playing golf and kept my mind off the painstakingly slow process of repairing my face.

Later on, I learned a few things that still seem impossible to think about. How did my wife and kids find out about my accident? Well, they were inside the airport terminal and would have had no idea what was happening to me over a mile away. A woman, an angel, came out of nowhere, approached my wife and said your husband has been in a bad accident and to please come with her. She took my wife and kids to the site of the accident and then left, never to be seen again. Well, there must be angels because I can think of no other explanation.

Being thrown through the windshield, how did I not suffer major eye injury damage? The doctors indicated the edge of my right hand and forearms had major skin damage and had taken the brunt of the force. There were glass cuts along the entire length of my arms. Possible explanation: my many hours of martial arts training kicked in and I instinctively raised my arms in a blocking technique that shielded my eyes. My right hand and outer forearms formed a framework that deflected some of the glass. As in many sports or skill sets you develop, repetition after repetition after repetition is drilled into your training so it becomes automatic, whereby your body reacts without you even having to think about creating a movement. I always thought it would be valuable in a self-defense situation but, in this case, it probably saved my eyesight. The key takeaway? Wear your damn seat belt!

I'll always remember my boss at the time, Ken Gifford, General Manager of the Sheraton Hotel, telling me he was waiting outside the recovery room when a kid who earlier had seen me being wheeled into the emergency room with a sheet over my head, asked my boss, "Is that guy dead? Ken's response was, "No, but always remember to wear your seat belt, kid!" Definitely good advice for us all.

My body was fairly battered with most areas badly bruised, in addition to a fractured jaw, broken nose, and a front tooth that needed replacing, but those 680 stitches in my face from plastic surgery were going to take some time to heal. To be honest, it was amazing that I was not injured more severely given the tremendous impact of a pick-up truck hitting me broadside at around 50 miles per hour. I was reminded of that powerful impact when small pieces of glass would surface from the back of my throat weeks after the accident.

The healing process was slow but my constant companion, Tanner (our lovable 75-pound Weimaraner), never left my side. Dogs are wonderful as they can sense their human's pain and want to give comfort and provide extra loving care, which can be an amazing gift.

Scarred for life now had new meaning for me, and I needed something to refocus my attention on. I had been working for the last six months on establishing a meeting-planners' customer advisory board to help our hotel and the entire meeting facilities complex surrounding downtown Birmingham to more effectively sell and market the convention complex and destination to the meeting-and-exhibition industry. In fact, our first gathering was scheduled in about a couple of weeks.

My friend, colleague, and mentor who helped set up this first meeting and established an agenda, David Dubois, was the President & CEO of PCMA (Professional Convention Management Association) at the time. He is now President & CEO of IAEE (International Association of Exhibitions and Events). David met with me while I was recovering and said, "You look like Frankenstein, my brother! Are you sure you want to do this?" I stated, "Yes, I started this process and would like to see it completed." Then I promised to sit in the back of the room so my appearance would not scare anyone!

David helped me complete the planning process and he spearheaded the initiative with the meeting planners. I stayed in the background with a crooked smile on my 680-stitched-up face, content knowing I had survived and finished something many people thought improbable.

Lifting 200,000 pounds in a 24-hour period does seem impossible, especially for a 66-year-old man; but sometimes when I explore and learn about other seemingly impossible feats…weight-lifting pales in comparison.

Adonis Lattimore was born without a right leg and

with a partial left leg, plus he was born with only a single finger on his right hand. His life was destined to be filled with heartache and sorrow, and yet he achieved something that cannot easily be comprehended and certainly seems impossible. This young man with literally no legs and one finger on his right hand won the Virginia Beach, 106-pound division, state wrestling high school championship! How was that possible?

As a wrestler in high school myself, I can tell you it was the most grueling and physically taxing of all the sports I ever played as a youth. Playing baseball and football was fun but wrestling took major conditioning and skill along with keen devotion to the sport. Those of us who competed in sports as kids know that all your body parts are needed just to compete at a minimum level. So how could this young man win a state wrestling championship with his severe disabilities?

It is easy to understand how people doubted Adonis could ever wrestle, but I read that he once said, "It's pretty motivating just to prove them all wrong and just to prove to myself that I can do anything I set out to do." It took six years of dedication and hard work before he told the Virginian-Pilot newspaper, "Really, if you work hard, you can do anything, even win a state championship without legs." Wow! Adonis's dedication and accomplishment are beyond belief. Somehow, this young man overcame seemingly impossible odds to achieve a spectacular result. I believe we all have that special something inside us, that once properly activated and inspired, can help us produce amazing things.

My brother once sent me a framed quote from Teddy Roosevelt, who said it best, "It is not the critic who counts, nor the one that points out how the strong man stumbled or how the doer of deeds might have done them better, the credit belongs to the man who is actually in the arena, whose face is marred with sweat, dust and blood…Who, if he fails, at least fails while daring greatly, so that his place shall never be with those cold and timid souls who know neither victory nor defeat."

CHAPTER 3

The Strategy: How to Attack a Seemingly Impossible Feat Through Training and Preparation

I must admit, initially, this idea to lift this massive amount of weight seemed improbable and perhaps much more than I should be attempting at the seasoned age of 66! But a lifetime of playing sports, and being competitive by nature, helped push me into thinking it might be possible (of course, many of us think we are always 25 years old and invincible…not quite).

I became a little more serious about my fitness and health and decided to hire a licensed physical fitness trainer to work with me over four times a month for six months. I wanted to learn more about proper techniques and overall fitness regimens. I worked out at LA Fitness and enjoyed the range of machines and free weights as well as cardio and overall equipment offerings. This happened well before I even thought about taking on this physical challenge, but it proved to be beneficial to my developing the right mindset and strategies to accomplish the feat. I also integrated yoga into my training regime, which helped with my flexibility, and I added meditation to keep my self-awareness and mindfulness sharp.

Thinking about how I could break down this training into manageable parts was challenging. I called my twin brother Bill who, after hearing me talking about this crazy 100-Ton Challenge and saying, "Are you nuts?" At your age you are going to break, tear or rupture something for sure." After laughing about it for a while, I explained that I wanted to break this challenge into three different training circuits throughout the day. He asked if I had thought about doing a night session, meaning sleep for seven hours and then schedule the final two sessions on the next day? Breakthrough!! I had been fixated on the components of a traditional day timeframe, as opposed to considering a more manageable process. This event would be a severe test on my body, so allowing for the normal sleep cycle would provide a needed boost to my energy levels and strength endurance.

So, the concept of three different sessions allowed me to envision how I could possibly manage that much weight while distributing the volume (200,000 pounds) over a specific period. Rest was critical to safeguard from injury. Instead of trying to perform this challenge over the typical day periods, why not incorporate a different strategy that would allow for a normal sleep time to reset the body rhythms and still be able to perform in a 24-hour period?

I think about ways we all try to tackle personal or business problems. We get stuck in a mindset that gets ingrained in our thinking, but in reality, it just takes a different perspective to help us re-energize and take on a new challenge. Whether it is a sales, marketing, budget or operational issue at work providing the challenge, or a personal issue weighing heavily on the mind, it is important to reimagine the perimeters from which we are viewing those challenges and chart some new pathways to gain a different perspective.

When I presented the 100-Ton Challenge to my friend Dana Cooper, he also thought it beyond our reach. But being a very dear friend, he encouraged me, and we began to review strategies that might work. We discussed the total weight and how it might be distributed over maybe three or four sessions. We then broke it down to 66,667 pounds per session (three sessions of lifting 66,667 pounds per session) and then into what types of lifts could get us to a number that was achievable without totally exhausting our strength or endurance levels. Dana and I discussed the concept of circuit training (picking a certain number of exercises, high-volume with a targeted manageable weight, incorporating different muscle groups done in succession). We reviewed a variety of exercises and the machines available that could help us reach our goal.

As in life and business, it is not very wise to bite off more than you can handle at one time, even when you feel very confident about your capabilities. Or when you follow traditional corporate thinking that says always give 110 percent (by the way, who can give more than 100 percent?!). Or Dana and I knew we could lift more weight on the exercises we chose, but also became aware of the fact that muscle fatigue was a real problem as well as potential injury if we did not spread out the amount of weight and the repetitions needed to meet our goal after each circuit.

Knowing your body is important in any fitness endeavor and understanding the stress and strain on different muscle groups and the ability to control and manage that stress is vital. We quickly realized that our biggest strength in this undertaking was to utilize our legs to maximize our poundage while trying to incorporate other muscle groups like our shoulders, lats, arms, and chest movements. In business, it is like assessing your staff strength and utilizing every employee's best talent to build a team that can perform more effectively and efficiently.

Personally, I am an introvert, but my mom always pushed me to be more social to develop other skills that might help me succeed in the future. Working the room was definitely not in my DNA but we all eventually do what is necessary and discover new skill sets. My venture into sales stemmed from my career stints in restaurants and convention services with the Marriott, Sheraton, and Westin hotels. This experience led me to land a position as corporate sales manager with the City Line Marriott outside Philadelphia, PA. To say that I was not a born salesman is an understatement, but I learned along the way to leverage other abilities, such as perseverance, tenacity, discipline, and the will to succeed.

The well-known English author and motivational speaker Marcus Buckingham has written many books about focusing on personal strengths. He is a leading expert and the world's most prominent researcher on strengths and leadership at work. He broke the rules and challenged the myth about always focusing on a person's weaknesses to improve their performance. Instead, he used research and data to prove that it is best to determine a person's dominant strengths and develop those traits to achieve significant results.

This is a strong reminder to leverage your obvious best talents and proficiencies, while always being aware of your shortcomings and working to minimize them. Obviously, if you are a poor speaker and are required to do public or company presentations, you will have to hone your presentation skills. Start by leveraging attributes that are fairly easy to develop, such as your energy, smile, or personal dress. Then go to people who are considered gifted public speakers and learn from them. Listen to their delivery and study their stage presence or other techniques that can help you improve.

The most important element of actually achieving the 100-Ton Challenge was having the proper strategy. You must have a plan…the right plan. Plan the work and work the plan, but only if you have the proper strategy. My original thoughts of lifting 200,000 pounds had to be broken down into more manageable segments. Eventually, it was my love of reading history and my fascination with the amazing nuggets of wisdom it can provide that helped me devise a strategy for our plan.

My favorite example about how a strategy determines the outcome of a major challenge, one ending in victory and the other in tragedy, is the quest to become the first men and country to reach the South Pole. The story of this true adventure provides excellent perspectives on strategy and planning. The following is an excerpt from an article about it written in 2013 by Brett and Kate McKay.

"In 1911, Roald Amundsen, a Norwegian explorer, and Robert Falcon Scott, a British Naval officer and explorer, both led expeditions to become the first to reach the South Pole. Both explorers had different strategies to accomplish this goal, and the results were quite devastatingly different. Each man and their teams had to cover over 1,800 nautical miles through snow and ice. Amundsen won this race and became the first man to reach the South Pole and returned home safely, while Scott found his way there five weeks later only to learn that Amundsen had already laid claim to reaching the South Pole first. Scott then tragically perished with his team on the grueling return trip home."

The article vividly outlines the different strategies taken and why Amundsen's plan carried out with methodical, disciplined consistency made all the difference. Amundsen and team skied and sledded five-six hours a day for an average 15 nautical miles, a distance that represented one-quarter of a degree of latitude. Achieving one degree of latitude every four days provided a motivating benchmark for him and his team. The key was they met that goal of 15 nautical miles a day no matter what the weather, conditions, circumstances, or obstacles forced upon them along the way. That plan, dogged perseverance, and focus made all the difference.

Scott had a different approach. He did not have a consistent goal in mind but allowed conditions and his own motivational feelings to dictate his pace. On ideal days, with good conditions and good weather, he would push his men to trudge nine hours a day, but when poor conditions and weather moved in, he would decide to hunker down in tents for those days, rest and achieve no progress. He continued to repeat that pattern, thinking he was maximizing their efforts and resting when conditions toughened.

Amundsen deliberately chose his pace and strategy to ensure his men and dogs were well-rested each day and not pushed to exhaustion, thus avoiding potential injury or sickness. Scott was impatient and thought you should always expand your effort when conditions were ideal, but he failed to realize that this strategy eventually led to exhaustion for his men and dogs, and on the return trip all died.

How did this example relate to my goal as well as my team's goal of each lifting 200,000 pounds in 24 hours? We knew that lifting too much weight in one exercise could strain or even injure that particular muscle group. Most guys like to prove their workout manhood by concentrating on the glamor lifts like the popular bench press, squats, and bicep curls, but in this venture that would be foolhardy. We could have tried to lift more per repetition, per exercise, but there had to be a balance and a plan to avoid muscle fatigue. You cannot push or pull that much weight in those types of lifts because doing so can easily injure or weaken the body. You must find a way to spread the weight distribution around numerous muscle groups. We had to experiment with different exercises, and then test out what we could max out with certain repetition ratios that could leverage accumulating enough poundage to achieve our stated goal.

The goal of 200,000 pounds could be broken down into three sessions of lifting a total weight of 66,667 pounds per session. We figured we could break these three sessions within a 24-hour period to give us enough rest between sessions to avoid injury and muscle fatigue plus allow for time for muscle recovery.

I am a big trial-and-error guy. Determining the right exercises was going to take some test runs. Certainly, having done a regimen of workouts throughout my life helped me assess some easier determinations in what exercises could and should be done in rotations. Your legs are a body's most powerful resource and would be our most vital instrument in attempting this feat. Our question was…what would be the most effective use of our legs and how could we best integrate that use into our rotation of exercises?

The concept of rotation and a circuit-training technique would prove to be critical in our strategy. I reference the explorer's example of their team's efforts and routines established in the quest to achieve being the first men to reach the South Pole. It was critical to maintain some sort of rhythm and momentum to achieve any goal. Whether it is lifting weights, selling for a living, losing weight, or tackling a personal goal, it is important and helpful to develop a consistent rhythm and, thus, build momentum. Think about a time in your life that you were most productive or successful? Did it seem almost effortless and just flow perfectly?

We tried to replicate that feeling…building a consistent rhythm or routine that creates and sustains momentum. Our routine developed into our circuit training technique of choosing eight separate exercises and rotating through those exercises in one circuit. I mentioned the legs being your powerhouse station. Squats are a popular and excellent exercise, but I had a fractured disk in my back, the L5 region, that prevented me from using this specific movement. The potential stress on my back resulting from trying to balance heavy weights on my upper torso, if improperly performed, could cause serious damage to an already weakened body part.

The seated incline leg press is an excellent alternative that I could manage and still balance a significant amount of weight while using my entire body mass for a stronger foundation. I started working out on this machine and learned I could perform a good number of repetitions, which was perfect for our quest of finding a core exercise that could contribute to maximum weight and rep ratio. I advise anyone attempting this type of challenge to prepare and train effectively.

In my youth, I was always fairly thin, so I became enamored with the Marvel Comics heroes of my time like all the Tarzan actors, Johnny Weissmuller, Gordon Scott, and Ron Ely. I played football and baseball and wrestled at 155 pounds in high school. In college I tried to make it in baseball but there were complications after I took an inside fastball that fractured my wrist. I also realized that hitting a curveball was tougher at the collegiate level. Then I discovered fraternity life with girls, kegs, hairy buffalo parties, intramural sports, and hitting the weights to look more buffed was much more appealing, so I quickly took my 6'1' frame to 230 pounds. After graduating and going into the corporate world, I trimmed down to about 190-196 pounds, which has been my weight for the last 40 years. I have always had to work out to keep weight on, so I have kept my routines consistent to maintain that ideal. I know, pretty damn lucky, but through the years I found staying in shape is easier than getting back into shape!

But about the seated incline leg press. I started training with single-leg presses at 150 pounds with 10 reps; over a three-month period, I alternated with the standard two-leg press at around 270 pounds. Then I went up to 360 pounds with 12 reps at a time for three sets and maintained that pace. I had determined that the perfect weight for this exercise was going to be around 270-300 pounds at 10-12 reps, realizing we had to do five circuits of all eight exercises at a certain rep ratio.

I continued my discovery phase at the LA Fitness gym to isolate and test various weight machines and determine the best combination of exercises. I must emphasize that using machines was the only way I could have accomplished this goal. Only superhuman, professional weightlifters or bodybuilders could try this 100-Ton Challenge using free weights (all dumbbells). The efficiency of using machines with balanced weights and allowing the mechanics of the machine to aid in performing so many reps was a tremendous asset.

Standing calf raises proved to be another exercise for accumulating a good amount of weight, so we added that to our circuit training routine. We realized that it would take incorporating all the muscle groups to ensure we did not overtax one body part. The back and lat muscle areas can be utilized to lift significant weight amounts, so we added a seated rowing machine motion along with a curl pull-down on lat machines, and then the back-extension machine also. Arms and chest needed to be added to round out our cycle approach; thus, we included a bench press and tricep pushdowns. The last exercise added was necessary to include the core area. We tested the abs rotation machine, which proved to be an excellent selection to make sure we really spread out the poundage and repetitions to a variety of muscle parts.

CHAPTER 4

Don't Ever Give Up…Just Reset!

Many tasks can seem overwhelming or just not possible with a normal mindset, but the ability to RESET is extremely important and vital to reaching your next level.

My friend Dana Cooper is an excellent athlete and sales-and-marketing executive with IMG sports marketing. Dana wanted to do something special on his 70th birthday, something that guys his age normally cannot imagine is possible to achieve…lifting 70 tons (140,000 pounds) within 12 hours and attempting to lift 700 pounds on a seated incline leg press and create a fundraiser to benefit wounded veterans. The fundraiser would again benefit the Gary Sinise Foundation, one of the best charities to support veterans and their families. Dana and I talked about training for this and reviewed our previous routines and regimens in accomplishing the first 100-Ton Challenge. The 700-pound lift is an extreme amount of weight, and you must be careful not to tear or rip up your knee or leg extremities in attempting it; this is especially important for older guys like us. I wanted to give Dana some incentive, so after training a couple months I went to the gym and loaded up 700 pounds on the seated incline leg press and attempted that weight. Damn, it was heavy!

As I attempted the lift, I could feel the extreme load throughout my legs, which were quivering significantly as though they might buckle. Yet, I found the strength to make the lift successfully. Knowing Dana's competitive nature, I sent him a picture of the stack of weights from LA Fitness that read, "Your coach did some recon and the 700-pound challenge awaits you."

We coordinated our lift days in late January and early February for his 70-ton challenge, deciding he would prepare to attempt the 700-pound leg press at the beginning of the exercise when his legs were freshest. He warmed up a little with light weights and then settled in to attempt this enormous amount of poundage. He had to back off after the first try because he experienced significant resistance and the weight hardly budged. He said, "No, this is not going to work." I knew he had the ability to make the lift, so I suggested he RESET and try again with renewed vigor, confidence, and energy… "Dana, you can do this…You've got this!"

He refocused and drove that weight up aggressively and accomplished his goal, ending with a big smile on his face. He then said, "Well, now we go on to the 70-ton challenge as part of my birthday celebration." It was a long day but after two separate 90-minute sessions, the 70-ton challenge was met, and Dana achieved both his goals. What was most important and rewarding was we raised almost $5,000 for the Gary Sinise Foundation.

It struck me how we can sometimes get stuck when facing a major challenge or obstacle. We just need strong encouragement and a RESET to accomplish any goal, whether personal or in business. The ability to focus, to visualize the result, and to try again is a powerful tool for facing any challenge throughout our lives. It takes preparation, it takes training, it takes perseverance, and it takes discipline, but the results will be worth the effort. You can achieve more than you initially believed possible... just retrain, reeducate, strategize, refocus, and RESET!

Testing and trial and error have always been a vital part of achieving anything in life. I am a big fan of Malcolm Gladwell and remember his blockbuster book "Outliers" as a resource for achieving mastery of any skill set. He described his 10,000-hour rule which says it takes about 10,000 hours of deliberate practice to become an expert at anything. Personally, I probably did 10,000 reps in training, so that book gave me some confidence! And it was all part of the discovery process of attempting anything new or challenging. The genius inventor Thomas Edison always thought that perceived failures, in his endless pursuit to make light bulbs work, were just steppingstones to success. My dad always believed that the measure of a person was not how many times they got knocked down but how many times they got back up.

Failure and recovery are wicked cousins, but that relationship is vital to crafting a path to success and harmony on the journey through business or life. It can be a lonely journey at times but one of self-discovery. In today's turbulent times it seems the most aggressive and brash personalities tend to get notoriety and attention. In reality, throughout history it has been the leader or individual who can bring a sense of calm, focus, and determination that has achieved some spectacular results.

It was a cold, clear and beautiful morning over New York City as the Airbus A320 took off from LaGuardia Airport heading to Charlotte NC, when suddenly the airplane struck a flock of birds, causing it to lose engine power. This was not a good start to a pilot's day! Capt. Chesley "Sully" Sullenberger and First Officer Jeffrey Skiles immediately went into their safety and backup checks to clarify their options. At the same time, flight attendants Sheila Dail, Donna Dent, and Doreen Welsh quickly went into their emergency preparation procedures. The sudden reality of this type of terrifying situation could create significant panic, even for well-trained people. Yet, these men and women quickly and with timely precision went through their checklists to see if they could restart their engines while also evaluating their options to land at the closest airport.

This tactic proved impossible due to the plane's low altitude and lack of engine power. The captain made the most important decision of his life, and the lives of his crew and the 150 passengers on board. He would attempt a risky and rare water landing in the Hudson River. This happened in January when the outside air temperature was 19 degrees and the water temperature 41 degrees, so spending any time in that cold water would mean instant hypothermia and possible death to those on board. Can you imagine performing all these tasks and analytical thinking within three-and-a-half minutes?! That is the total time it took from takeoff to the water landing to complete "the miracle on the Hudson."

Just think about how you have dealt with any overwhelming challenges in your life or business. What was the first thing you did after panic took over? How were you able to gain control and potentially steer the situation back in the right direction? Or did you stay in panic mode and lose control? What could you have done differently? Capt. Sully and his crew's actions resulted in a safe landing, and saved 155 lives, which from the outset seemed improbable. Maybe we all need to take those first brief minutes of a crisis to assess our own situations, go through our own checklists, and see what options we have for our own personal safe landings…or, at least, start crafting a path to help improve our chances.

A checklist might have saved me some pain during a trip to Salt Lake City when I thought mountain biking (for the first time) down a 5,000-foot single-track path was a good idea!

I was finishing some business in Salt Lake City that provided me with the opportunity to enjoy the great outdoors with my friend Scott Beck, who was CEO of the tourism agency Visit Salt Lake and an accomplished cyclist and athlete. My plane back to Tucson did not leave until late in the afternoon on my day of departure, so we pretty much had the whole day free. Scott recommended that we go for a mountain bike ride. I had done some road biking but never really ventured into the mountain biking arena. I thought, how could it be that much more difficult? You could say I was about to get a life lesson in resetting my athletic prowess.

Scott picked me up and we began to drive up a mountain on the outskirts of Salt Lake City. We drove, and drove, and drove until we got to a turnoff at the top of the Mill Creek Pipeline Mountain Bike Trail via the Rattlesnake Gulch Trail. We got out of his SUV, and I saw he had our bikes and all the gear prepared and ready to go. I thought this looked like fun, but it was definitely going to be different from any road bike trip I had taken, where most paths are fairly flat with some hills.

We started out and he said to just follow him and watch out for some rather sharp turns. At first, the path was kind of flat and followed some solid and compact terrain with beautiful scenery along the way but keeping up with Scott was my biggest challenge. As the path started to get steeper, I was thinking it would be paramount for me to keep focused and really take it up another level. I was losing sight of Scott and obviously I did not know the trail at all. I got about half-way down to where Scott was waiting for me. We had planned to traverse down the steepest part, but first he wanted to regroup and give me some advice. When I reached him, Scott was barely out of breath, while I was feeling a little winded yet building up the confidence that eventually would be my downfall… literally!

Scott did warn me that some of the trails down the single-track trail coming up would be a little more challenging. He said I should especially watch out for one of the tightest hairpin curves, which could be treacherous. I thought I was getting the hang of this mountain biking stuff and was ready to handle it. I was really focused on just trying to keep up with Scott and at least keep his bike in sight. As usual, he was easily way ahead of me, and I was losing sight of him, so I tried to take it up a notch and sped down the trail. A big mistake.

I saw the tight hairpin curve turn coming up but thought I was prepared to take it on without realizing the high speed I had built up. Unfortunately, I had to hit the brakes much too fast for the curve and, consequently, I made it only half-way around. I jackknifed over the handlebars and down a 100-foot cliff. It happened so fast, but I caught a break, so to speak. My body was hurled over the cliff, but fortunately my fall was broken by me hitting a tree about 15 feet down from the edge of the trail. To say I was stunned would be an understatement!

Immediately, I felt some pain in my left side and my left wrist, but I was glad to be on solid ground at least. I found myself at the base of a tree, on a hillside with some dirt and shrubbery among rock. I looked to my right and saw that the ultimate cliff was about 10 feet away and it dropped about 100 feet down into a ravine. Damn lucky I hit that tree! Cascading over that cliff would have been life threatening.

I looked up to see the edge of the path and thought I better start crawling back up. I started to make that crawl, but the loose rock and dirt made it more precarious than I imagined and slowed my progress. I tried to carefully grab whatever I could to make the climb back to the path. Unbelievably, the bike was still in good shape but the knucklehead riding it was pretty beat up with scratches, torn shirt and pants, and a bruised ego.

Talk about a RESET! Have you ever had a time in your life when you felt inadequate, embarrassed, and downright stupid? Clearly, my ego far outweighed my athletic ability on this bike, plus I was told in advance about the treacherous potential curve ahead. Yet, I did not prepare myself for that challenge. How many times in our personal and professional lives have we been warned about something but did not give it the proper attention? Or maybe we just were not willing to do the preparation to make that goal achievable, or even downright resisted the help of a friend or mentor? We sometimes need to set aside our egos or past thinking and be prepared to take on new challenges but with a different mindset.

I knew I was only half-way down the mountain at this point, and it was sort of remote, so finding additional help could be problematic. I got back on that bike and headed for the trail to try and catch up with Scott. He had stopped about a quarter mile ahead and was waiting for me. When I finally met up with him, of course, he said, "What the hell happened to you?" And after seeing me up close, added, "Well, I told you about that hairpin curve!" When he asked how I was feeling, my adrenaline kicked in and I said that I had some cuts and bruises but was ready to go. In reality, I was feeling the pain, but I was determined to keep making my way down the single-track and just see how I felt as we went along. Scott took it easy going down the last half of the trail, which I appreciated, and we finally made it back to an open parking area that I thought was the end. Wrong!

Scott said the SUV was parked another mile down the main road, which was really steep so we would coast all the way down. For that I was thankful. But I must admit that it was pretty scary racing down the road at around 40 miles per hour on a mountain bike, not knowing what was ahead. I thought…Damn, I just survived being jackknifed over the handlebars of this bike and potentially being catapulted down a 100-foot cliff, and now I was barreling out of control down a mountain road at high speed. Well, at least this will make for a good story.

Boy, was I happy to see the end of that road and to get on flat land and comfortably inside his SUV. Of course, there was the next question. Should I get checked out at an urgent care center before heading home? It was 1 p.m. and my flight back home to Tucson was at 4 p.m. I thought I could get a late checkout at the hotel, take a shower, and make my flight. Scott was skeptical but I said that I was sure. He looked at me curiously but agreed to drop me off at my hotel. Getting out of the SUV was a struggle as my internal injuries really started to become apparent. I went to the front desk and asked for a late checkout but was denied by the clerk. My pain was getting worse, and I probably looked like hell and was not in a good mood. I requested to see the manager who eventually came out. After I explained my condition and situation, I believe she felt sorry for me and granted me two more hours.

My left side started to stiffen, and my wrist and rib cage were on fire. Making it into the shower was an ordeal. I literally had to take off my clothes with one hand, but the warm shower felt great. I knew I needed something to reduce the pain and took numerous Advil to get some relief. Getting dressed was another challenge, but I eventually managed to make myself somewhat presentable before going to the airport. I crawled into a cab and finally made it there, but the plane was delayed. Now what?

Well, the Advil was wearing off and I needed more immediate help. I wondered what one of my boyhood heroes, John Wayne, would do. Well, I found the bar and ordered a shot and a beer, and then another, and then another. The drinks helped ease my pain until I got back into Tucson and went to collect my luggage at baggage claim. By then the pain had really kicked back in, so I said to my wife at the time, who was there to pick me up…I think I need to go to the ER!

Not my finest hour. As it turned out, I had three cracked ribs and a fractured wrist. My body eventually healed, but the process was painfully slow. Lessons learned can be hard, but I certainly mastered the value of doing a RESET in my life. And my dad's sage advice to IMPROVISE, ADAPT, AND OVERCOME came in handy once again. Plus, now I know if some guy named Scott Beck invites you to go mountain biking…be prepared!

CHAPTER 5

The Results and What's Next?

Training for the 100-Ton Challenge did not always go as planned. Some days, I just felt sluggish and weak; other days, I was sore, and the weights felt extra heavy. Occasionally, I did not warm up properly, my technique was poor, and I would tweak my back. Then I would have to rest a few days or even a week before returning to my normal routine.

I always had the August 14 date in mind because that was my dad's birthday and mine was August 15. So, the end goal of performing the 100-Ton Challenge on those days was always paramount in my mind. Raising money to honor veterans through the Gary Sinise Foundation and dedicating the lift to my dad's memory was a powerful motivational tool. As that day came closer, I started to accelerate my training and test my endurance and strength. The strategy was clear, and we had a definitive plan to achieve this seemingly impossible challenge, especially at the ripe old age of 66!

My son Matthew, friend Dana, son-in-law Colin, and I all agreed on the specific eight exercises, the specific number of reps per exercise, and the specific number of weights. This formula was designed for us to handle efficiently and endure the five circuits over three different sessions for a total 1,230 reps over a 24-hour period. My thought was to at least try to achieve three circuits of all those exercises, weights, and repetitions on my training days. I wanted to see how that felt and then build up to doing super sets (two sets with the same exercise and repetitions) as I went through the entire circuit. Doing super sets would essentially accelerate my maximum output in a potentially shorter amount of time, usually resting about 90-120 seconds between each exercise.

Some athletes like to ensure they can achieve running a full 26 miles to accomplish finishing a marathon or cycling 100 miles to achieve the century mark in a competitive bike race. My approach for this challenge, since it was never attempted before by any of us, was slightly different. I knew it would take a significant toll on our bodies to lift over 200,000 pounds in 24 hours, and I especially did not want an injury to sideline any of us before the August 14-15 target date. Of course, my training regime allowed me to feel confident that I could do this, but I wanted to leave a little bit of gas in the tank to create that essential extra motivation and good fear to reach this unknown territory.

I felt strong and in good shape after testing my ability to perform at least three or four circuits in a single session, which gave me great confidence. I believed I was ready for the big day. Other key elements to my preparation were proper diet and liquid intake.

Keeping hydrated is always important and I discovered using BCAA (Branched-Chain Amino Acids) was key for me during my workouts and certainly through the time of the 100-Ton Challenge. My brand of choice was called XTEND Original BCAA powder, which provided 30 servings per container and zero sugar. This product helped me with muscle recovery and electrolytes, and it was easily purchased through Amazon at around $26. (FYI: I get no compensation from any company I mention in this book. I just want to provide honest feedback on what has worked for me). My recommendation is to test various brands and find out what works best for your metabolism.

Protein intake is also important, so I make sure to get a good supply throughout the day. This is especially important for men and women over 50. Some of my favorites for protein are chicken, eggs, almonds, pistachios, Greek yogurt, salmon, peanut butter on rice cakes, avocados, and raisins; bananas are a good source of potassium, which helps the body before and during workouts. I have also added Whey Protein Powder drink mix, which comes in a convenient package and is simple to mix with water or almond milk.

Undoubtedly, most people will experience some significant soreness and muscle aches from this type of weight training. A friend of mine, Mark Hansen, recommended trying a supplement called Isotonix OPC-3, a powerful antioxidant that helps with joint flexibility and muscle recovery, and supports cardiovascular health. I took one dosage in the morning and one at night while training over three months, and it definitely helped me. This product can be bought online at www.shop.com.

When August 14 arrived, everyone was excited to get on with the big day! I had coordinated with the Gary Sinise Foundation months before the event to structure a fundraising website that could easily be sent out as a link. The website explained the mission of our 100-Ton Challenge and was designed so people could donate directly. Thanks to a great staff member, Logan Allison, who was the development coordinator, the website was easy to set up. It tracked our progress and provided important information about how the monies raised would be spent. We hit our goal of raising $5,000, and that gave us additional motivation to go out and lift those 13 elephants and that Boeing 737 airliner!

Matthew and Dana coordinated our pre-event schedules. We agreed to meet at my house at 5:30 p.m. to get fueled up with a home-cooked meal. My son-in-law Colin Buchanan lived in Denver, so he was planning his lift times close to ours that night and the next day. My lovely wife Catherine, who is a fabulous cook, prepared a superb meal that included skinless chicken breasts with broccoli, baked in a lemon and olive oil sauce and seasoned with parsley. We planned to allow ourselves about 90 minutes to digest properly before heading over to LA Fitness to start the event at 7:30 p.m.

I made sure I brought my 24-ounce bottle of BCAA mixture to keep properly hydrated, and I suggested my training partners do the same. To keep us focused, we brought along a copy of our training regimen, which outlined the exact exercises and number of reps. We had scouted in advance the busiest times and days at LA Fitness to ensure we would have access to the right equipment without potentially having to wait too long for our turns and lose our momentum. An additional strategy was to have one of us jump ahead to the next piece of equipment, so we could get in the necessary reps on that machine while maintaining the integrity of our circuit training routine. We started on legs first, and with a good pace completed three circuits before we started to experience a little fatigue and tightness. Then something happened that I had feared could derail our collective efforts to achieve the 100-Ton Challenge.

My son was getting too aggressive and trying to accelerate his movements through the circuit training. He became slightly fatigued and lost his form and technique, and then he suddenly experienced extreme pain while performing the back extensions exercise. This was a major problem since the back is a key foundational structural muscle group for most lifting movements. We stopped to assess his injury and see if he could continue. Matthew was definitely in pain. He said he could continue and gut it out but would need to eliminate the back extension machine and try to replace it with another exercise. We recalculated a leg exercise movement for him with the right number of reps to keep him on pace with the needed amount lifted to finish the session with 66,667 pounds. I give him a lot of credit. He showed some true grit and was able to complete all five circuits; but, of course, the two old guys had to give the young buck some significant trash talk about keeping up with his senior partners. :)

When Matthew got home, I made sure he immediately iced the injured area and took some ibuprofen. Splitting up the event's 24 hours into three sessions, which included using a night session, served to be a godsend (thanks to my twin brother Bill's suggestion when I originally discussed taking on this challenge). This plan allowed us to get a normal sleep cycle in before coming back the next morning to complete the second session really crystallized and reinforced the importance of proper preparedness, planning, and strategy.

How many times in our lives have we attempted to change jobs, lose weight, repair a relationship, plan for retirement, or even improve our health without a well-designed strategy? How did that work out? Maybe you met with early success, but it was not sustainable. Maybe the results were disappointing, and you became frustrated. Maybe it was a complete failure, and you were devastated? These types of results have probably happened to us all at certain times in our lives, which only reinforces the importance of resetting, and structuring a new plan or strategy in preparation for what comes next.

The next morning came. We met at 8:30 a.m. to start the second session of the challenge, which went great. My son had a strong recovery and, although he felt some tightness in his back, he was ready to go. Dana and I were eager to attack the second session and launched into the leg, lat, and rowing machines. That first 290-pound inclined leg-press exercise felt a little heavy this time around, and I began to think how we only had 133,333 pounds left to go!

Next, we then traversed to the pulldown and lat machines. The muscles certainly felt tighter after completing those reps and a slight amount of doubt started to creep into my mind. Then I recalled the story of my dad making his way through the jungles of New Guinea for over a week, after escaping from his Japanese captors to get back to American lines. I thought if he had taken on a war to serve his country, I could handle a little physical pain to achieve my goal and honor him. The rest of the morning session went fairly smoothly, and we finished in around 90 minutes.

It really helped that the gym was relatively open that

morning. We were able to get on all the machines we wanted without skipping around to accommodate other gym members using the same equipment. I had spoken to the manager early on about the possibility of isolating or reserving a set number of machines on our training circuit, but he said that was not possible. So, we had to adjust occasionally by getting on machines we had targeted that were open and available. We had eight separate exercises outlined on our training circuit, and we could always find a couple of machines ready to be used so we did not lose our momentum.

The third and final session that afternoon was more challenging. We all felt some tightness and fatigue settling in, and the lactic acids were building up quicker in the muscles as we progressed through the final session. Another stumbling block was that the gym suddenly became busier, so our rhythm was broken at times, which meant we had to jump around to secure the machines needed to complete the five circuits.

As we faced these final obstacles, I reflected on why we were doing the 100-Ton Challenge and the inspiration behind it. First, to honor my dad and his outstanding service to our country. Second, to honor all veterans through the Gary Sinise Foundation, which builds homes for veterans who return home after suffering severe injuries from combat, including many who have lost arms and legs defending our country and now need our assistance. Sometimes we need to put our own challenges in perspective and find a renewed strength to forge ahead. Those types of sacrifices can never be forgotten or taken for granted.

Every muscle in my arms, back, shoulders, core, and legs became instantly stronger. I was revived to pump out those final reps, the final circuit, until suddenly we had accomplished our goal. We had lifted 100 tons, or 200,000 pounds, in 24 hours. We all shook hands and hugged our exhausted bodies. Our plan, our strategy, our discipline had worked! It may sound a little strange after lifting this massive amount of weight, but I felt I could lift more, like I had some gas left in the tank. It was not as hard as I imagined or perceived. Maybe this was an omen, a message that we all have a little more to give when it is for a worthy project, an inspired goal, or a dedicated mission.

How did we celebrate? We went out to a good Italian Restaurant to carb up and have some beers and pasta, of course! We met up at a very traditional, classic Italian restaurant in Tucson called Bazil's and then started the feast. I must admit that first beer and bite of pasta smothered in old-style marinara sauce was tasty and memorable. My wife Catherine had found us a good table and we had a wonderful evening. As we finished eating, we congratulated each other and felt a strong sense of camaraderie and achievement…then I thought, "What's next?"

Well, unfortunately what was next was COVID-19.

Who could have imagined the toll it would take on everyday life. Lockdowns, masks, social distancing, economic turmoil, massive cutbacks and job losses. The devastation was fast and furious and became a global pandemic quickly. We all became homebound and had to learn a new way of life. What can you do? What were your thoughts and reactions? This was unprecedented for our generation, thus there was no real road map. The Spanish flu epidemic was over 100 years ago, so the treatments, medical practices, and protocols used then were archaic; but the sense of isolation, rapid illnesses, and millions of deaths remained the same. Closer to home for me was when my older brother passed away from COVID-19. Unfortunately, his illness was expedited by his underlying COPD (chronic obstructive pulmonary disease) condition.

My family and friends were critical for my mental and spiritual strength. We all relied on each other for support through constant contact (virtually) and caring. At the same time, there was a lot of downtime that had to be filled with something. This situation had the potential to become positive or negative in a very quick fashion. Keeping both physically and mentally fit was extremely important. Going back to the gym was out of the question, due to statewide restrictions. I decided to buy some workout bands online and start a new routine at home to maintain some level of fitness.

This helped me remain focused on something I knew could assist in supporting my own immune system should

I contract the virus. Keeping mentally fit was another matter, but I also discovered that you could take classes online at edX, from some of the world's best learning institutions like Harvard and MIT, for free!

It is easy to start wondering about all the political rhetoric and divisive discussions related to the cost of education. Yet, we have tremendous assets online that can help bridge the divide of providing education to all Americans, regardless of economic status, at low cost and from the comfort of your home. Yes, there are some costs like access to a computer and proper internet connections, but there are programs to assist with those costs for those who have the desire and the will to pursue that road to achieving an educational degree.

Lifelong learning has always motivated me so I found that you could achieve many certifications online and because of my interest in fitness and health, discovered International Sports Sciences Association. This forced isolation period afforded me the opportunity to become certified as a fitness trainer, sports nutritionist coach, senior fitness specialist and a health coach.

The pandemic forced us all to live and think differently. I discovered there was light for those who could somehow RESET and redirect their energies and thinking. Reading helped me tremendously, and I became fascinated with individuals who overcame severe obstacles to achieve what some people thought impossible. John Morton-Finney was one of those individuals. Here was a black man, born to a slave father in Uniontown, KY, who became one of the first Buffalo Soldiers, a member of the U.S. Army 24th Infantry Regiment. Morton-Finney also served in WWI with the American Expeditionary Forces in France; survived the Spanish Flu Pandemic; became an educator; earned 11 academic degrees, including five law degrees; and lived to 108 years old, and actually practiced law up to his retirement at 107! His personal motto was "I never stop studying, there is always much to learn. When you stop learning, that's about the end of you."

We can achieve more than we believe or perceive is possible. There is greatness within us all, but we must be willing to seek it out. So, I again asked myself, what's next? What could I do to make a difference?

Sitting in front of our warm fireplace, enjoying a cup of hot coffee with my wife, feeling blessed we had our health and had avoided COVID-19 (although we both became very ill in January 2020 and believe we may have had an early version, which, in hindsight, may have helped our immune systems combat the virus later on).

One day, my wife and I turned on the CBS Sunday Morning Show and learned that 20 million Americans faced unemployment, and a record number of people faced eviction notices and worrying about how they would put a roof over their heads and feed their families. Many of these people were part of the travel, tourism, and hospitality industry which I had spent 40 years of my life working in with many colleagues and friends.

This struck me hard because I knew this industry would be hit the hardest and devastation and hardships would be forthcoming. What could I do to help? I remembered Gary Sinise's words, "You could always do a little more."

Why not try another 100-Ton Challenge and donate the monies raised to benefit those needy hospitality workers? I was healthy, still fit, had the road map, the plan, and strategy to achieve the 100-Ton Challenge. I could lift those 13 elephants and that Boeing 737 airliner again and use that platform to inspire people to give a little more so we could help all those hard-working hospitality workers who were facing some significant hardships and challenges.

As always, though, to achieve something special, I needed some good partners. I thought about a professional acquaintance, Brent DeRaad, who happened to be CEO of my former employer, Visit Tucson, an organization that promotes, sells, and markets the destination around the world and who works closely with the hospitality industry. I explained my mission and desire to give back to some needy hospitality individuals and families in the Tucson area, and he jumped right on board. Plus, he had the connections and network to identify who might have the greatest need and even volunteered himself to participate.

At first, Brent thought he would just agree to lift a portion of the 200,000 pounds as a way of showing support personally, but then I explained my strategy and game plan with a detailed outline, and he became more excited about the potential of doing something far outside his comfort zone. Brent was in his early 50s and a good athlete, but never attempted something of this magnitude. He thought more about it and said, "Let's do this!" and became fully committed. Of course, my son jumped on board. He grew up being exposed to the hotel business due to my career and he has a good heart and wanted to pay it forward again. In addition, my son-in-law, Colin Buchanan agreed to join us remotely, so the team was formed.

We started training in October to be prepared for the attempt on the 100-Ton Challenge in December. Brent helped create a webpage via his technology department, headed by his webmaster Hope Smyth, who did a great job creating a homepage that could be integrated into a Go Fund Me page. He also sent a message to the hospitality community, and we identified some needy individuals, which was not hard, especially since it was during the holiday season in early December and there were some very deserving people: (1) a laundry attendant at a local resort furloughed since April 2020 who had been injured severely in a recent car accident; (2) a housekeeper at a hotel furloughed between March and September whose daughter had passed away recently from COVID-19 and who faced large medical bills; (3) a family whose husband and wife both lost their jobs due to the closure of a local attraction and faced tremendous hardships.

Anyone not motivated by these heart-wrenching

scenarios would need to check their own purpose or priorities. We were truly inspired to attack this particular 100-Ton Challenge and, hopefully, make the holiday season a little brighter for these hardworking hospitality workers. We targeted December 10 and 11 to complete our mission, and everything went smoothly. We used the five circuits and the eight different exercises with 10-12 reps, each over three sessions within the 24-hour time frame and it went like clockwork. Our ability to have pioneered that routine gave us the game plan and confidence to achieve our second 100-Ton Challenge. Breaking through a perceived barrier certainly paves the way to future success and accomplishments.

There was a time when the four-minute mile was said to be an unbreakable record. Scientists and doctors of the era stated the human body was not capable of running a sub-four-minute mile. Yet once Roger Bannister broke that barrier and recorded the historic time of three minutes, 59.4 seconds in 1954, the record was broken again 46 days later. This seemingly impossible feat has now been accomplished over 1,300 times since then. Thinking about it, you begin to understand that the power of breaking through perceived impossible challenges to make them achievable takes a different mindset.

Most important, with our second 100-Ton Challenge, we raised over $8,500 that went directly to the individuals and families we had identified as most in need. I thanked Brent DeRaad for his participation and coordination of the event and for his willingness to provide a small sense of financial relief for those hospitality workers. Handing out those checks was most rewarding. While I wish we could have done more, it felt like a million bucks to have made a small difference in the lives of these hospitality professionals.

This book has helped me gain a deeper appreciation for what is possible if you carve out a new path, reset your thoughts and attitudes, chart a game plan, and structure a new strategy with the conviction and inspiration to go beyond perceived boundaries. My advice: seek out open-minded friends, colleagues, and partners who will support your dreams, your aspirations, and your ideas to challenge the status quo and even take on a perceived impossible task.

Enlightenment and courage are all around us. I was watching the recent ESPY (Excellence in Sports Performance Yearly) awards ceremony and listened to Dick Vitale (famous sports broadcaster) deliver a speech after accepting the Jimmy V award for perseverance. He outlined his views on what it took to be a winner in life. He spoke about the four Ds: Desire, Dedication, Discipline, and Determination. He then added some additional ingredients with his three Ps: Perseverance, Passion, and Pride. Wow, that just about covers it.

Each of us may have our own personal brand or code for taking on life's challenges, professionally or personally. I have used the Zorro brand concept of making your own mark in life. But I believe the key is taking the time to learn, seek out, and discover what is possible and to chart a specific course and strategy through educated trial and error to achieve your desired outcome. Greatness is within all of us …we just need the WILL to discover it!

In his book, "Hearts Touched with Fire," David Gergen recounts how Viktor Frankl, a survivor of The Holocaust, "poured himself into a book recounting his experiences. In only nine days, he wrote his 1946 bestseller, 'Man's Search for Meaning.' In it, he concluded that the difference between those that lived and those that died in the camps turned on one thing: meaning. Those who found meaning in life were much more hopeful and resilient. He argued to other prisoners that they should stop asking what they could still expect from life; instead, they should ask what life expected from them."

Powerful thoughts that can help all of us try to reach a little farther, stretch beyond our perceived capabilities, achieve things that the naysayers say is impossible. Turn the phrase from…"They said it could not be done" to "It can be done!"

Thank you for taking the time to read this book. I hope that I was able to provide some insights that may prove valuable in your life, at any age, and remember to always try to pay it forward. You can and will make a difference!

PS…contact me at ravzorro@gmail.com if I can ever be of assistance. Wishing you much health, wellness and success.

APPENDIX

The Magic Formula for Lifting Those 13 Elephants or a Boeing 737 Airliner!

Over three sessions (consisting of five circuits of eight exercises during each session) over a 24-hour period, 7 p.m. at night, 9 a.m. the next morning, and 2 p.m. the next afternoon.

Each session of 66,750 pounds x three sessions = 200,250 pounds.

Seated incline leg presses
300 x 12 = 3,600 x 5 circuits = 18,000

Calf raises
290 x 10 = 2,900 x 5 circuits = 14,500

Back extensions
130 x 10 = 1,300 x 5 circuits = 6,500

Pull-down curls
115 x 10 = 1,150 x 5 circuits = 5,750

Seated rows
115 x 10 = 1,150 x 5 circuits = 5,750

Triceps pushdowns
110 x 10 = 1,100 x 5 circuits = 5,500

Abs rotations
110 x 10 = 1,100 x 5 circuits = 5,500

Chest bench presses
105 x 10 = 1,050 x 5 circuits = 5,250

Total: 66,750

Fitness and Health Accomplishments:

Achieved International Sports Science Association Certifications:

>CFT: Certified Fitness Trainer
>
>SFC: Senior Fitness Coach
>
>SNC: Sports Nutritionist Coach
>
>CHC: Certified Health Coach

Achieved: 100-Ton Challenge in 24 hours twice, at ages 66 and 67

Achieved: 70-Ton Challenge in 12 hours at age 68

Achieved: Lifted 700 pounds on seated incline leg-press at age 68

P90X Graduate

White-water rafting: Colorado River, Rogue River, Snake River, Salmon (Upper and Lower), Middle Fork, Kern River, Arkansas River and Youghiogheny

25k and 50k cycling races for El Tour de Tucson and El Tour de Mesa

Golfed around the world and enjoyed hitting some of the top-100 golf courses including: Bandon Dunes, Pebble Beach, Cypress Point, San Francisco Golf Club, Olympic Club, Riviera, Medina, Merion, Pinehurst, Torrey Pines, Firestone, Southern Hills, Los Angeles

Country Club, Lake Nona, St. Andrews, Royal County Down, Royal Troon, Turnberry, Muirfield, Carnoustie, Gleneagles, Royal Dornoch, Royal Portrush, Royal Birkdale, Royal Liverpool, Royal Lytham and St Anne's, Ballybunion, Lahinch, Waterville, and Old Head.

Made in the USA
Las Vegas, NV
09 March 2023

68818953R00046